THE PACIFIC NORTHWEST POETRY SERIES

Linda Bierds *General Editor*

THE PACIFIC NORTHWEST POETRY SERIES

2001 **John Haines** *For the Century's End*

2002 **Suzanne Paola** *The Lives of the Saints*

2003 **David Biespiel** *Wild Civility*

WILD CIVILITY

David Biespiel

University of Washington Press *Seattle and London*

Wild Civility, the third volume in The Pacific Northwest Poetry Series, is published with the generous support of Cynthia Lovelace Sears.

First Edition

Copyright © 2003 by David Biespiel

Printed in the United States of America

Designed by Audrey Seretha Meyer

08 07 06 05 04   5 4 3 2 1

Library of Congress Cataloging-in-Publication Data

Biespiel, David, 1964–

  Wild civility / David Biespiel.

    p. cm.—(Pacific Northwest poetry series)

  ISBN 0-295-98351-5 (alk. paper)—ISBN 0-295-98352-3 (pbk. : alk. paper)

    I. Title. II. Series.

PS3552.I374W55   2003

811'.54—dc21

2003050736

The paper used in this publication is acid-free and recycled from 10 percent post-consumer and at least 50 percent pre-consumer waste. It meets the minimum requirements of American National Standard for Information Sciences—Permanence of Paper for Printed Library Materials, ANSI Z39.48-1984.

www.washington.edu/uwpress

FOR **TRICIA** AND **LUKE**

CONTENTS

PREFACE

The poems in this collection represent two years of writing almost exclusively in a single form. The form is my own variation on the sonnet, a nine-line sonnet, what I've come to call an "American sonnet."

The prototypical line for these nine-liners is decametric (though, as free verse variations, the lines vary, some more & others less than ten metrical feet). These sonnets are shorter than their English counterpart by lineation, nine lines versus fourteen lines, but longer by sound, one hundred & eighty syllables versus one hundred & forty syllables.

Regarding the speakers of the poems: Imagine a Coke bottle, shattered & whole. If the whole bottle represents a single unified voice (my voice, say, my core lyric voice), then the shards of glass are fractions of that single voice. In this sense, the speaker's dramatic voice in each poem represents a fragment of my voice—a lyric fragment, that is, that gets just nine lines to speak.

To my surprise, the result has been a kind of explosion of language. I've drawn from the vocabularies of history, science, art, sport, philosophy, religion, literature, government, domestic life, etc.—often within the same poem & in varying registers of language.

I've come to imagine the nine-line sonnet to be like one of those classic Thunderbirds, something distinctly American: wide, roomy, & with a robust engine.

DAVID BIESPIEL

WILD CIVILITY

PAGAN

On a *shabbat* morning when I used to live without straining for
    deeds, I awoke sleek as a man in a novel
Who was blunt, who mumbled, who adored the slovenly, the
    punitive and vile, and who exposed his loins to nubile girls.
In that sleep-world I was a pig, a glögg-head, a fearless man-
    child. I knew my navel
Better than nectar. Flagellation was my vitamin. Not one
    serenade, not one salve, to save me.

But it wasn't me. I was a tumbler, a night-crawler, who couldn't
    look a woman in the eye
Much less a girl, for fear she'd see me lost by choice, like a
    negligent lion. Here was a one-man
Network of the jussive, a ganglion, who needed the tribal and the
    frat, a self-made legion of inquisition.
Bereft, I locked the t-bar lifts. And the pièce de résistance: a cyst
    for a mind, a vial

Of scotch. Godless, I loved and listened like a crow to the chortle
    of rain. *G-o-d*, that sound, was my nest.

HALLUCINATION

Mushrooms

Dotted-and-raised, strutting, like Braille, we transformed our
    blood into rigs of nipping swallows, and flew
Into evening's quick ink and fiddled on the swing-set jetties and
    ribbed the fibrils of light
We saw everywhere—in unyoked oaks, in the eighty-five eider
    ducks, in the delinquency of tidy bliss,
Crying *Gee* or *Haw* as we sought out grave and hive in the logic
    of the juvenile hedges

That sometimes disbursed, harum-scarum, in our eyes, harsh,
    shrunken, like greening murals of hush.
The fire sirens were harsh grifters. The air was a prank of prayer.
    Sometimes we hung in the branches
Like Burroughs' Tarzan, sometimes like Lords of Surrender. And
    then surgically coming down, limb by limb,
Sterile and stalled, like the brain's gray orb or the heart's rescue,
    we bounded, laughing, into the survival kit of the kitchen,

While the counter-tops destabilized, and the floors stuttered, and
    the coats on the veins of chairs cried for more.

What We Thought, Peaking

Let us stampede with our presentiment. Let us pantomime like
    an emancipist. Let us nap as spies nap
And give up nagging the meek. They're bereft as parents above
    the incubant. (It's all normal
As wood, dire as wood, sunk, and enisled as wood.) Let us wager
    with each thorn
In the spastic horrors of daily love. Let us not be ghouls. Let us
    not trifle in the narthex.

Let us praise, instead, the merganser. Let us scan, instead, the
    pace and path of the moccasin-wearing boys
Who disdain laudanum, who dislodge the sterile singing, and
    swim in the freshets that come after frost.
Saddle up, friends, we're off to snag the germs of shrift and scam.
    We're off to sink
The holy Rx, the meristems of post-Icelandic longing. There's a
    candle to light

For every feather you find, every gram of edible nasturtium.
    Bring your candelabra, friends. The miracle oil's burning.

The Widow Bird Trip

Gradually I blossomed (sitting in the branches), and in merciless,
    scattering flecks, poured out my creamery,
A slavish spool. Tubulous, haughty, a wad of Percy's mill-wheel
    sound, the craft
Was scat. I could've called for Osage dances—or been the
    sundew trapping their brains—
Because where was the falconer, faker, freak, crazed with smut,
    to stop me?

I accrued like a savior's dreams. Opposite the appeal, the
    cyclopic, isotopic
Sacrament of remembering a crass loss up in the summer
    leaves—open-handed as the nude, odd as a code—
I was an illative of late damp air or fever. (I was Mopsus where
    moss
Was concerned.) And my Mrs. was spleenful, pursuing her slurs.
    And the brew was drab, and the battles

Were folly. I puckered in this valley of streams, open-handed as
    hope, odd as a pun.

Cult

These days I long for the kakistocracy of rub and touch, the
    personnel of pleasure once struck-out for
Before the lash and snag, before we were weaseled and scolded.
    Times I stand in the mirror now to see the ruins
Of the body, half remembered, I know not to think I was a foil,
    neither nation nor prince.
I was a thug of a dream, a fool's follower, a bawling stoner. My
    pretense: to know thunder

And anger, fire and love, to know them deep inside the body
    before they disappeared
Into the hot distance. Sheltered from the crass, the stricken, the
    kooky blare of bells, the pabulum
Of newsreel, we knew the sworn-in, fey, off-year reefer, rolled up,
    like pupas, and toked. Our loose telepathy
Was pithy as kisses. We misdiagnosed and powwowed with the
    whip. How I loved the scar's burn

When channeling to the Paleolithic core of the self—flogged,
    mesmerized, smug, like a converted whore.

The Mystic Trip

All night my dreaming armies hunted without luck for
    immortelles. They locked out hookers, and on tenterhooks
With the coronets swearing *Sing, Sing, Sing,* they trampled the
    unlettered mire. They sucked immune pathologies of the
    lowdown
Like leeches, tainted by light, negrophobes of burn and grief.
    At Mont-Saint-Michel,
Nauseated in the thinner airs of transcendence, they got snared
    in their maskless phrases. Such imperfect contrition

Seized one would-be ex-dreamer, and his impromptu rape
    brought the locals to shame.
While once in Montpelier, Vermont, we only braced for the terse
    freaks and deadheads (there's the difference
Between exile and vacation). There, Lysippe has her eyes
    blackened. Here, the Skinner box is the new naturopathy.
    The gloss
Is the goal, lathed with pastries and aloe. And the pastoral
    theology of craft is hocked in the pre-fab coffeeberries—

While the proper lochia is left on the sheets, and the tentmaker's
    wife begs to die in her own bed.

UNDER A BLOSSOMING PLUM TREE
—Labor Day, 1996

Under a blossoming plum tree
In a summer of peace,
Tallying the steps

The gang of jays made near the blackberry-
Entangled roses, I thought of the glassy
Distance between loved ones—

A river without a bridge,
Dying lilacs
In the merlot bottles.

What the Earth means—
The dirty crabapple leans down

Crippled more
Than a windblown candle.

Like murmuring
Old men

Fearlessly bowing
Their heads

To the eternal flame,
The apples keep falling

Bruised for weeks
In the humid grass.

Once waking at night
My lover beside me,
I watched the slick grass
Sputter: the heart's like that—
A wick in a drafty window.
I'd awakened
From a dream
Of a black room
Filling with water.
My lover beside me,
Her eyes like chicory.
She was swimming
In and out of
The tumbling waves,
Turning her head
To open her mouth
To the actual air.

Inside the vinegar bottle
Is the Caribbean.
When I turn the glass
Upside down
The imprisoned sea
Tumbles, pounds,

          and settles
Like dust.

When I hold the ocean
In a bottle sideways

The bubbled air
Stops still:

This day, the next,
The purpose,

The work,
Is language.

What if Uncle Rueben hadn't said a week before his 97th birthday
That he didn't believe in god, because where was god
When the Jews were holding their six million last breaths,
And I said, how do you account for it not being seven million,
    fifteen million, fifty million?

FRENCH KISS

He never had a psychograph to fetch the sagging gripes of the
    sufferer. He was ripped with suffering, pummeled,
A prawn of manpower. And yet for all his droning in the mouth
    of the gynarchy, and though he sang
Praises to the soul kiss, it got to be a chore, a jerk of the groin,
    and he got so frail he withdrew like a hurt moth—
A scene in a play (seen now or by crowds a hundred years hence),
    that moment came and went.

So he turned to a lectionary of runts, but without triumph.
    Instead, the marvelous vanity
Festered and shut down like a fenestra. Then a darkness rose out
    of the mind's bubble—with a guileless pipit crying *Modernist*
    America is dead and gone.
And when he thought to try again on the bed of arch and strafe,
    when he thought that life was worth the threat of life,
And his dreams broke inside his head like sparrows and dancing
    was the sorrow of pilgrims and beggars,

He suddenly feared that silly sketch of easy-blown theater could
    disappear again like his centuries-forgotten mother tongue.

POETS

William Butler Yeats

I liked best the desolate nights that rained the color of slate and
  mimicked complexities of cats and kings.
Also, unseeing eyes. The sun helped no soldier. It never broke or
  slaughtered fear or changed
The winds or damaged mavournin muse with her unforgiving
  beauty. Whining gave tenure to generations.
They should know—playboys of petty summary. Passion,
  precision: I wished most to know these fraus

(There's desire worth residing in). I feared to pull back, aging
  into spongy italics, but the torn accounts
Cackled like pulp. My method was not unlike the meter maid's:
  Here's to our kingdom of shape and spades.
And now I see the hunters rush from the shore with spiccato
  nerves, and their erotic ilk,
Outfitted with hermetic eggs, still fated to dance like guards in a
  metier of red berets. I long for a pub

With a few pints more, to be leg-less when debating artistic wiles.
  There's a Spica worth sailing for.

Robinson Jeffers

These human affairs the passenger pigeons huffed at. No mare
    nostrum between us or a drag on the head
Like Caligula's dream, no lace in the veil between the eyes and the
    outside world. We got spangled
About as often as we got delirious. I used a loupe to decipher
    some poems. Then regressed into the ligaments of waves,
Creaking, wracked, racy, grunged and gassy, Ledan with a wail of
    sun or, up at the predawn mountain shore, sullen as haze.

There were blasts and stabs. The trespassers never made it past
    the snug stone, ton on ton of it, lugged up here with the
    boys,
Work that sapped the seconds out of the hands. The sea gulls
    were august. The crews of mariners, the mariculture of ice
    plant,
Left us unrouted. *That old shaman* one girl said behind my back.
    Here's to the Ramadan of cliff-dwelling,
Here's to the lessor in each of us, and the ledgers we keep our
    famine-feared numbers in, each pugged and huffy,

A lesion of ones and zeros and sevens, the energies and sagging
    gear of our bodies, the minutes of glom and strut and fart.

Miroslav Holub

What I said outside the House of Knowledge was I did my best
  writing in prison and for a period thereafter when a gnat had
  more identity
(Though following through the streets were the government
  SUV's with their windows tinted black). I was a grunt, a
  stringer,
A sabreur, not a rebel. To curtail pricks and bruisers, they
  thugged the puny. There was no predestination, nor wrath.
It wasn't drastic. You didn't have to be fanatical to give offense:
  their surreal meant the world went round the sun.

Stranded, jaundiced, I could neither answer nor escape. (The ana
  seems vaunted now, but it was salmi
Only, an elm not an island.) Caged, yes. Spackled, yes. A culprit,
  grist for the rich, a non-person, yes, all this.
What did they know of Ariadne or Hamlet's tooth? Denuded,
  effervescent, sprung from the briar,
Once I puckered up to a general's wife and sprained my lip. I
  rubbed the bruises in ink.

The trepidation was lame. Nudged and stripped down, I limped
  not to die.

William Stafford

Traveling through the darkly winnowed towns and the dirty
    counties, snagged in the grainy breaths of strangers
And the sass of trains, without an unsigned message from a
    migrant sage, and carrying my box of candles
And knapsack of needles through the dales and the barn dances,
    with a knack for games and regaining ground,
We came upon the straggling gaps of Colorado. Looking back,
    East, mother's flat wind

Called like a light snow. And though I sounded back with my
    best bass voice, and though I began to tell
Stories of being lonely on the trail to big dreams, unguided,
    smothered by the bullets of duty,
Or suddenly lost in grim childhood where my own children
    would fib and puff and thrum
And go away, as children do, searching for their own crook
    in the Peace River. That's how I wound up at the nearby
    bend with a blue-eyed muse,

Where the low waters spoke to me, hesitantly, the name
    Hutchinson, a word, often unheard, under these
    far-western moons.

DEAR JUSTICE

I'm getting to forty like a roughed-up toy stranded in a firing line
    of pastimes. The mortgaged house
With the closed rooms swelling with lavender, the oiled mitt and
    whiffleball and bat by the scuffed door,
The mithridate that is rhythm and dream only—these are the
    ingredients to be endeared to or die for,
These are the rites to swig, though I could no more understand
    them than solve the witch of Agnesi.

An agnostic man has no hatchet face, no mitzvahs of faith, no
    chants to summon with an edgy twang,
Crying *dang* the way some cry *shotgun wedding*. I've a nice knack
    for cynicism.
Down to the follicles, down to the air a ball rips through in pitch
    and catch, I'm all folkway, sloping like a father.
That night, over bouillabaisse and the last of the wine, we played
    your "Closing Line of the Film" game, and finally I won

With *Breaker Morant*: Shoot straight, you bastards. Don't make
    a mess of it.

EXPLICATION DE TEXTE

Here's a tribe of shackled rats in the Lake District section,
    hosanna! The brute utterances
Squashing the safety of happenstance. And more, rattling over
    here, the noose of the possum who's a kaiserin,
Crazy as a spot. Time rubs its tables like a silent butler. Here's the
    safe knot of a chance medley,
Pliant, ladled, the festoonery ratcheted a notch, busted, edited.
    I'll re-read. OK with the sun.

Red Warren, rest-in-peace: That year we were broke it took one
    1963 penny to save the heart from typeset.
Had I skipped even one cup of coffee, I would have never seen
    each digged-up iota jump the track.
Once, hunting the mismatched pages, I had to cry: *Quick,*
    someone, who is the Chancellor of the Exchequer?
You need one good eye in this business, an accurate arm, and a
    heart without control

To be no taller than a devil or, like a safety catch, to find the
    adage, the words, hosanna.

FAITH

Cosmography

Had I a pseudoscope to see the inmost speck of heaven as posh
    fortalices of light
Or even to map mountains of the awesome oceans that store the
    west-south-westward trickle of winds,
Then lets them go, like a forthright gift, level and wet, a fright to
    undo the odors of subtle lifting, then I wouldn't need any
    instrument
To call Kali. (What is it with creation and destruction?) Heaven is
    in the head, baking in that small oven like birthday cookies.

Some mornings it takes ox-tongues, it takes the pre-show release
    moan of an actor, to measure the yawp of skies.
The cosine won't help, nor Politburic knowledge. The equites are
    happy in the gymkhana. They lurch in bright tights and
    bandannas
And seem to rise off the wood flooring like the grace of the
    morgue's smoke. Even that political economy,
Like the stakes of the Gypsy, are cursed—the hex is set, the winch
    twisted shut. Feet, stay put on this black earth,

This kaleidoscopic ground that sinks like a field's navel. Such
    doves are sudden, unglued by more raving sinners.

Natural Religion

Suddenly I saw the ice bulletin blink like a lantern (and the lice
    were climbing across the table),
And the lookout called in with the flu, and his backup staggered
    out of the lockshop—
He couldn't outwit a nucleotide. There, in the dream world of
    twill and wilt, I was a gliding monoplegic,
A dunce without a leotard, a clod mugging to join a clan of
    hocus-pocus devotees.

And I took to calling *Guide Left*, and I took to digging and
    wading through tough floods.
Freewheeling, I was more of a heretic in a hermit kingdom of
    germ and mock REM.
I could glean lunacy in any moon where the end-runs, suddenly,
    are end-stopped.
And when the runt of my fever quickened, only a towed skiff
    could get me to the light of faith.

All this, despite the godless fiasco that needed mopping up before
    my disappointed rebbes came home.

Demarcation

And the dividing line of a life is between chamber pot and
    chalice, between crud and creosote,
So that the hours of gathering old-man's-beard in a basket makes
    you no more than a file clerk for toads.
And the dividing line of death is between intrinsic and instinct,
    between the threads of the infinitive and the finite,
So that peace will come only as a piperonal that leaves a land ripe
    with certainties.

And those who live with despair stop where the dwindling wind
    stops,
And those who live with memory endure in the dwelling places
    of their ancestors,
And those who live with hope scrunch their hearts in irk and
    guilt and luck,
And those who live with ignorance are attentive to the preaching
    that quibbling is joy, and those who live with joy

Are like a man who digs a foxhole against the drab war, believing
    it's a bed to make love in with his girl.

GENTRIFICATION

—Hawthorne Boulevard, Portland

I'm worn out with these stud desserts. They leave me dysphasiac
    as a father. The descant is snide.
(Where is the antsy dynast now, that golden eagle dreaming of
    Elgin marble
Like the golgotha loaded with grit?) The shops keep coming past
    39th Street. Antiques and wine bars
Overtaking the auto bodies and head shops. The gentlewomen
    with their flag-draped prams

Morph into foggy homographs. Foul-tempered, trumped with
    pills, cringing in fragmented Muzak
Of cunning, they're a horde of determination, a faction of
    musique concrete.
They snort their ounces of Ouija as if sniffing sunlight when,
    or if, it comes. And yet is this
The way we will meet, pleased to be the other's rag? Is this the
    way we trade our drought of kamikaze youth,

Out of earshot of the busking violinist, as his music, like the
    dervishes of order and odometers of ohm, goes mad?

AFTER THE WEDDING

I hear the wood slats wince on the back porch
And leap at the spruce bough's mid-evening bend
The way I heard it weeping during the vows
While a cardinal jumped from spruce to pine,
Settled for a low branch in the day's union,
Its backswept crest a four-cornered fold,
The sharp conical bill hard as a nut-
Cracker. Its muscular black was full and
Ethnic across the face like the wind's
Brush on the air through the looped
Crest and spindle gaps on the rocker. Then gone
Without a whistle. Then the sway,
The long wooden pulse and throb, the rutted
Boards' plumage hard as wind under the wing.

DRUNKS

Maneuver

He wallows in good fellowship, slung over the mild wine. He
    vamps at a cool distance
Somewhere in the corner of the crowd. He won't get his feet wet
    in the bun fight.
Inertia of the brain, his timbre. He's a featherhead, his loam is
    untilled, and his long suit is vanishing.
He won a feel-good shag, that's all. He embrocates and gargles,
    a looby, vaporous, chlorine-drunken medic.

If there were a loan translation for his stratagems, it would be the
    priest Laocoön.
Warning against the Trojan Horse, he failed to keep the serpents
    from killing his two sons. Here's a warning:
The gregarine are thieves, scheming, parasitic, in his blood. The
    cancer's coming, just ask his people.
He shouldn't get riled, clap his hands, or sit on a hat. No manual
    to learn malevolence, even in ravines of onlooking.

He should look tall, nod, smile, peer into the retina of the
    sloshed human eye. Each conjunctiva burns. This, his luxury.

Misdemeanor

After the maximum blame, after the mumble and grease of
    loving her like a queen,
Then, after, loving her, unrequitedly, after the manner of a
    struggle
Or dream about the strangle of debt, decimal by decimal, when
    all he can do is embalm the fear
Or plea, studiously, in a plaza of annoying destroying angels
    (with a heaven of vendettas

Like a destiny, a blab of the unevenhanded), only then does he
    take the concrete drill home
To dig up the driveway and install the rolled-up lawn that's no
    less enchanted as a silent memory.
There's no tribunal for loss or losing one's way. Gangly, glum:
    he put his neck out.
If only there were a lap for him to put his head on. It's what he
    does best

When convicted, lying there, barefoot, his head on the grass,
    rebooting in the gamboge of the light.

With Codeine

Ill-starred, dream-nettled, smitten, timid, hands fat as gloves,
    the riddles shrill as a lariat,
And now, looking in a mirror, bellowing—*Here I come to save*
    the day— he strolls and strolls
The back fences of recurrences. Jovial or vague, even on gravel,
    his legs feel gyved. Now it's a groove
Of extemporaneous prancing. Now he's a timorous emperor
    (without pretext or lifeblood),

Lewd, delved-into, flabby, aphasiac. He files one by one behind
    himself, sure to derail the drill, to lie
About his dolorous sniffling. He's a dealer of capers, a one-man
    coop, an oompah with the blood of needles.
He edifies. *Short, short, short, long, long, long, short, short, short*:
    To pocket the glowing
Decal of his head, it takes a code to break, to save himself. What
    he hears, bristling with an undressed treble, phat and bold,

Blonder than a nilly, doubles as atrophy—a trap, a buttress,
    a siren, like a diva, dripping *coo, coo, coo, coo.*

CIVILITY

From that place in the imagination, wild and without ornament,
  where the mutts are rock-ribbed
And mutable, and the tulips are musty, it was better for him to
  plant thyme than to know himself.
The repeating decimal of temples was a pal. The last time he
  visited the half-retard cook, his cousin,
The feed-through was robust. There were fetishes and heuristic
  seductions. The dogs got what was left of the Seders,

And when he took up with geodesy and sought to understand
  poverty's gestalt, he never looked back
Or called his mother. True, omphaloskepsis got him through
  fifth-year Greek. The layovers, the revolving voyeurism,
The dreck and bribes and muddy codes, the pins in the lantern-
  shaped maps with their bright grids:
These he grafted like tattoos onto his pythonic heart. Fed up,
  he could crumble like a ruined house.

And the thistledown, and the tuffets of the dug-up work, these
  brought on politer screams.

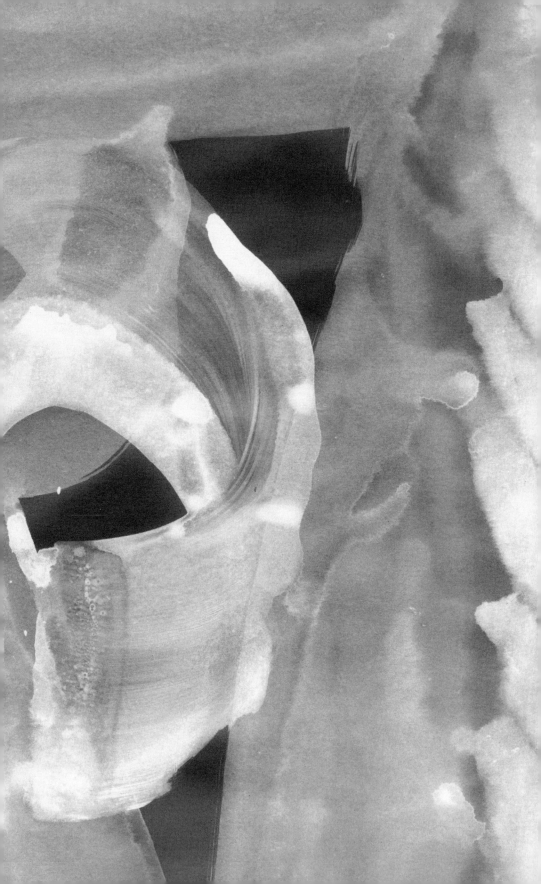

SHOULDERS

When I hold your collar,
Clavicle, and blade,
It's like holding all
The waters of the world.

The brown pelicans—
Their sweeps clean
As a bone's curve—
Don't care.

Nor the gulls
Picking bits of char,
Nor the sullen-faced
Day moon.

Your long-distance letters
You signed Penelope.
The sun, the sun, the sun.
It sounds like waves,

Love, turning.

BRAWLS

Third-Generation Immigrants

We were like Bedouins. We left the household arts south of any
 hurt. We were not signatories to ecologies of slavery.
We bought no Federalist blunderbuss. We hadn't stolen the
 hellebores. Often times, stratified like hellcats
In detention, we feigned injustice. We kept our dinky god in the
 brim of these fedoras like one small flaming rat (Dionysus
Understood). That's where the refund for sleep came the year the
 baby's breathing turned sour.

We needed grit and the lead in our blood when our old-style
 heralds said *Scurry.* At last we had to stay put,
And that day in the schoolyard, when Ratinov had me pinned,
 I had no idea that econometrics of rebellion
Would, over time, turn into an indent of memory. Got to be
 willing to hit the other guy first—
Never grith enough. Even now, with the bluebird poking at the
 planters on the deck, the old dog rolls the bone

Round its tongue. And the new generations go on searching for
 one innocent thought.

Appanage

Now in the first wind of autumn I can say something extra to my
    enemy without panic of choking,
Without meanness or disdain, but with empathy, with geniality,
    so that my enemy
Can feel the visionary enamel of the words, even from this city of
    two rivers that roar out from the forest
Like two fierce winds leaping in a ruckus of prophecy, palpitant,
    flexing their liquid muscular airs.

You slop-work of a man, you slug, you're so lax. You're a crock,
    a lemon. Even your wife laughs
Behind your back, laughing at your self-love and all the crap
    about the legendary you—
You're the husk and not the corn, the commentary and not the
    text, the shell, the old skin, the meaning without the
    experience.
And this will be the story I tell to my children in bed, a kill-shot
    clean as crystals,

Of the big bad apple fallen before the rains come: Come, cheer,
    as it sinks into the soft grass forever.

Winter

Soon it will be over, though the rains and war go on. Decency
    calls for a cadence, like needing a pinafore,
Ass, neck. No one clips the panicle. So much for exposition.
    A pox on sinning.
(Where's the English sonnet? It takes one mask of cosmetology
    to hide from the rosy noose, to swerve from glom.)
Where's the nonsense verse knee-deep in the diphthongs ding-
    donging in the padded air?

Soon the cynosure will be a shine of spit and song. The distaff
    will give up on additives.
Somewhere in the new grass I'll crawl around and suture the
    pure and declaim scripture
And scrape the reports of battles from newsprint, despite who's
    winning.
The legends of the beautiful world are already rescinded, and the
    seasons squeeze tighter than a gymnast's pike

And spin like radio static. Now it's Fats rinsing the Rebs from the
    icy creek. Hurrah for this glut of blood.

SANGRIA

Security of prayer, perk and brace and crib of the cliff, wide of
    soothing: I found the lake and rowed
Toward a glimmering wind. Without my vulgar Latin, I lacked
    the diplomacy to gloat or turn to velvet.
The chum, my host, I called to: *Come within an inch of the sloppy,*
    prigged regality.
Later, I hitched across trusses. My theme was to dote on method.
    How many years,

Wandering like a proxy to a mother, has it been since I touched
    that water's beard?
Once, despite drink—red as a mote, rust, red as a shirk or
    manifest perforation or rain, red
As the hotter fixes, like sweat or a ringing in the ears, without
    a target to pray for
Nor Torah to pocket—once, despite drink, and beyond the flop
    of bottles, I scribbed and sniffed the unending roses.

The tips of those nights were softer than a second's tick, luber-
    ous, even good, like a failed sect of yum-yum.

XERXES

I found the grunge and their overstuffed pulks, and the magic
    cups sculpted and sold by privateers. Their travails
Pent up inside me and tormented my sleep. I could've splurged
    on the marginal. A tap behind the eyes was a meltdown.
Dog by dog we bullied on. My thrill was the white-faced whistler
    at my side. He kept my spirits.
And the women hiding behind their infants, we left them to their
    razed wits. It was stellar, I tell you,

A dulcet of little fixes, a footing with dignity, the dimpled, tough
    we, inheritors, bezonians.
I loved the izars of women, I loved the shock and luck of the
    women, even when they nulled me—I was voracious with
    rape and the whip.
No parliament could repatriate. There was no leniency. The
    gestation of it, the base hate of it, the tut-tutting
I heard in my mother's voice, *What limit?* she said, *What limit?*
    So I'd call the whistler to soothe me,

To mitigate the stall, then the dogs would howl, and we'd soldier
    on with the lovely war.

PRAYER

Twenty-Twenty

This morning I'm standing as far away from my people as I can
     get as they mingle in the temples I loved once,
And I see not them but my own body, one by one, standing and
     swaying, from right foot to left foot, and sitting down, again
     and again, all of my stomachs empty from fasting,
My best clothes uncreased and smelling unworn, with lack of
     care, on this day of forgiveness,
And when my vision warps, I get fainthearted, giggling, aghast.

This dream study is so hard on my head. It's like the torn shirt on
     the clothesline, waving prettily, though gnarled, like a
     mirage, in the wind.
There's no hang-tag to tell me of life's composition, how to care
     for and use it, and whether or not to do right or wrong.
Meditation is out: The world is a trance, in gigantic high fidelity,
     clear
From head to toe as it is from far out among the stars we don't
     live around—this blue eye spinning,

The little time there is here for any of us believers and unbeliev-
     ers. That's all that matters on this day, as on other days.

Kol Nidre

And then to be dessicated again, praying on both feet, a clinker
    among the forgotten cliff-dwellers, a lughead with casual
    awe,
Unable to decide on esteem or, like Ossian, satisfied with
    dwarfish tragedies, fasting on a metal tray of ice.
Further on, the clunky jewelry of evening was a rinky-dink peep
    show. Then the cantor got colicky,
Lobbing the umpteenth note, like an ossifrage or sign of stars,
    over the heads of the drowsy—

And the umbrella trees were cradles of reverie, and the Guv said
    Remember there was no wheat at the kolkhoz.
I needed a pep pill right then (you couldn't get it on the Sister-
    hood's goniometer). At last the voice for god
Pennied in my good ear, first with *kakeeeyaaaah,* nicely, in that
    colony of tag-a-long.
Timid as a young leaf, sure, and fastened to a rib of creeds, I was
    the ram, too,

Nibbling on the fringes, feeding on the uncoded message.

Latitudinarian

Why should I be convulsive, vocal, a canal of indirection? I didn't
    deplume the others, mule-deep and en masse
In their race course of devotion to the one story. I'm OK with my
    hang-dogged body, febrific, hoof-bound.
Even my rapport with the godless is point blank. I'm good for
    drooling and plosives and foolishness. Got the Polaroid
As evidence. Times like these it's best to dally and avoid the diner
    on a fasting day, to give up

Frijoles (they're too rich for heroes). One thing I lack is a master
    plan. My steeple is stale and the smock
Too small. It tugs at my neck like the sound of my name. For
    another thing: All my joss sticks are dented.
Come the future, I'll drive my gypsy cab, think about the length
    of old goatees,
And keep a brick on the pedal. I'm steering out of this tunnel,
    cheerless and unaffiliated.

That lightning ahead is the shaved horizon. Despite meddling,
    it neither lapses nor pleases.

STARLINGS

Thus all the starlings rose into the netting of rain

As if they could learn from their own shadows

How to twitch, how to give up their wings and tracks.

They rose like rapture over the high crowns of fir

And spruce near the rivers where unspeakable love ended long

    ago

And the volcanoes hadn't yet awakened.

They rose over the downtown cranes

One sees gleaming, at evening, above the glass and steel,

Straining their necks over the new city.

Thus all the starlings rose on strings of air.

It was all you could see, standing on a bridge,

With an uncovered head, gazing through the dangling drizzle.

They mottled and spread like hysterical vines.

Flashed and wished themselves into the sky.

EXILE

The barbed wire is a comfort between my clumsy house of bread
and that Sukkoth.
Ill-gotten, untutored, un-Christian: Those muscle-bound
homesteaders mourn for their old-world breeds.
They role-play with mulled wine as it spills round their feet and
ankles, up to the knees and testicles,
But does not kill them. That's what the vodka's for, an ostinato
that slums within seven degrees of wisdom.

These days I've scalpeled the heteroplasty, relapsed, been
trapped, fuddled the full-blooded difficult ones
But didn't grow luminous, didn't fluff with my race, didn't enjoy
the Roman holiday or the multisensory laws.
These days I think of the life-and-death summers still to come
and the eternity of solitude
Minus the scrubby minions. From here, as the last light of
another day of looking away from brothers dims,

I can see my old man's hardware—what kept his immigrant heart
ticking—lying on the table, saved, like a rock from the
moon, in the Ziploc bag.

GODHOOD

So much of the parabiosis was split at the forefoot. So many
    things, like miracles, bleached,
So many things less sultry. I'd think of the sly burn of the age
    and remember the slow gulls and their independency above
    troughs.
We threw pennies at their wings to dent feathers (the wind came
    back at us with its vague acid),
And yet so many things no longer fit in my one glove.

Then the new rules. Crossing the Equator meant piercing an ear.
    Everything else—algae, nonce art,
Turf, smut—was inconstant. Even common things, like dapping
    in mid-ocean, became no better
Than knowing a mind reader's secret. I couldn't keep the farragi-
    nous sulfur in my head.
So many things were go-go and hazard. My teeth were bees. The
    stumps of my gums

Grew unsatisfied with their luck. My low-spirited body got
    indexed as a monument under Myth.

FERDINAND MAGELLAN

It wasn't far from Spanish crust, those large and garbled waves.
    They bragged in streaks.
And the overt torrent. And the secret ovarian light that plunged
    and toppled our sails like a prize.
Not that we were lathed in light, but our spirits, much of the
    time, wanted the occult of the sun,
Wanted the flag of the lotus, that drunken respite, deep in the
    soul of all that was stark, in that middle.

East of there, feeling a sensitive visitation, we knew, too far out,
    we might never come back
To preserve the ten reversals of fortune. A viper in the intestines,
    like ice sighing on the eyes,
That was what we felt, out there, ocean-lonely, our only staple
    the wind. No stipend to rely on
But the fire that was in us like a compass of guts. It was impossi-
    ble to sleep nights. Easier in the daytime,

Even in the stinging assaults on hope of the weeks-on-weeks of
    stranded stillness.

PARTIES

Scrum

He wouldn't be caught dead in a leisure suit for that hack and
    rant and scrotum-grabbing game,
No humor to it, nor honor, among that crowd, and plus they all
    got sulky and skunked in defeat, sloppy,
And lopsided, decadent, and iffy. *Semper fi*, one screamed, like a
    legislator of tin-pan,
Crying (*those fucks at the bottle*), with his rugby babe's panmictic
    mating hump he boasted of.

I remember one night one easy bloke, with a good set of teeth,
    put his head through a door at Richie Doyle's house,
And Richie, in kind, prancing in a sod-caked English jersey,
    cussing through every other word,
Wobbling with his pandurate body, heavy with tequila, ranted
    and rapped him across the face
Eight, nine, or ten times with his ring-fattened knuckles. The wail
    of pain was parched from so much beer—

He was laid out in the lawn like a toad in that condition. It was a
    plausible game, as the women paraded over his body and
    cursed his mother.

Passeul on the Roof Deck Above Glenville Ave.

It could have easily happened by the salley gardens, among the
    plummy leaves
And the blue-black berries of the myrtle that are never trim and
    have a mystic plumpness to them.
It was a mystery where her high style came from like the canned
    point of view of the second person,
A higgledy-piggledy scamp with plumose legs, a National
    Guardsman's trigger.

A twirl, a filly, like a late bouquet of creeping zinnia, dwarfed and
    trailing,
One-eyed in the basket, she was a flirty pastel of a nova, a votive
    novelty, begging: *Either you love me or you hate me.*
Whether she was a reproduction of a duchess who bequeaths
    vittles to peasants or a novice with sprockets for feet,
Dead on the lam, she didn't need to steal her snow-white mask of
    hard labor with the hardhat screwed into her skull.

She was daring the edges, shining like the wacky felt of light from
    her safety lamp.

SPIRITUAL GUY

Now in this spring pall, among the dour rhododendron and the
    unbridled goslings,
I stand with the loiterers outside the secondhand shops.
Orange-faced, stubble-faced, saved by retail as if it were public
    verse, saved by the freaks who lack a pick-off move,
Saved by the half pint of stout and the old-fashioned field days,
    I'm a solo foursome, white as the last rice.

I'll be coming, count me in, with my peewee songs and folk
    dreams, husking my gushes as if husking the sky.
I've got the talent to gnaw and can plug a loop. I won't be
    chicken of sketches. My gallop is all romp. I'm the most
    positive man in the room.
Even if this overhanging wind is drier than a beacon with
    nothing to prove, I've got my dirt memorized.
If anyone dares to squeal thinner than a newborn, dares to reveal
    that rage drives their imagination,

I've got my anecdote ready. That sapling in my front lawn,
    it knows how to accept what it gets, whether it's sun, wind,
    or rain.

BRUSQUE

I have known coarse emporiums of speech, have scrubbed and
   browsed with a tongue that lies like a melting lemon.
The emollient tremors in my mouth were not ancient. They came
   only a hairbreadth away from the hackneyed norm of the
   times:
That soft, looping, alphabetic wishing and formless grail of
   screwed wanting and desire and needing to know
How much one feels about oneself. The charm of the monger,
   crimes of love, all the while repaying the roiling IOUs: these
   were called the Plain Style.

I have read the outpatient stories, their row upon row of stones.
   Nearly all the outermost storms of this planet have claimed
   the names of women—
That morning, in Gloria, battening down the roof's deck was the
   only way to ratchet down our norm. Our qualm in the 90-
   mile wind
Was to mull the red-hot muck, to practice recuperation, as if it
   were a tracer of rut. The shrill wind,
The lavish punt of wind, like the Earth's dream of water buried in
   a desert hill—I came upon it like an unknown city

Rising out of a sloshing wrath of language, what even a quarter
   note of speech can't track. There was a blessing that couldn't
   begin too soon.

ARS POETICA

Epileptic

Always there'd be the stoic necessity that sucked the troubles dry,
    and, maybe, baking in the brain
Like a harlequin, a quarrel good enough a sign for blood to cradle
    through the hours and save me from the spell
Of swallowing the tongue. How brawny, errant I'd be. The
    episode a requiem (like an insect's stinging sliver
It seized my sleeping neck). Then all at once a noiseless gush, a
    splicing blurt of charm—though charm's not what it was—

Gauze of nerves, dizzy stroke, a jigging operative kowtow, the
    eyes like craggy currants,
The body seized by heart and throat like telling someone you're
    in love you know can never love you back.
A needle in the eye—my prayer to puncture and destroy the
    curse.
Sometimes it's hard to know what's worse, the way convulsions
    tear the tongue or these minutes in between

One madness and another—the sunny, dust-impending stir,
    the icy air and everywhere-awaiting fear.

Catharsis

Right here I'll stop among the nubby bunchflowers and the rats
  that look on, without flinching,
Scrappy in their whiskery sheaths, and I'll go nowhere anymore,
  and build nothing.
I'll take this bog. It's gettable. Forget chastisement: no martyrs
  need apply for the trademark (that poet
With his voice, it's the only one he gets). I'm golden, open as
  summer, alone with the peacocks (spare us further practice,

We'll hang onto our nugacious pearls, some for the duma of
  alms, others to shun our gushing days—
They come gradual now). These hours are whelped like a twelve-
  inch ruler across a skeptic's knuckle.
I can't modulate that gibber. No one skedaddles. Skewed, dusted-
  up,
Worked tighter than a fever, some nights I'm the dirty thrush
  whistling all the way to Ulster.

Those striations of song are spittles of an unskilled heart. What
  I'd give to undo that luck.

KAZOO

Not that we were troubadours but we could *yak*. Elite blowers,
  no. Our hurly-burly had no pedigree.
We were a barrel of moon codgers, funky as a rash, susurrous,
  flaming, unplugged.
The *whah-whah* was antenatal, a tenuous bort. We *hurrahed.*
  Our cadillo made lacquer dry—
We startled with *harpies,* we reclined, rose, with the *blurts* and
  reals. Not caustic, but battered.

The one calculus of it all: our tongues were fancy candles. They
  kept the burn going. We could *star-spangle*
Or heave *our-father-who-art-in-heaven.* Furled or unfurled,
  rigid or grand prix, sorry as ashes, shorn as flan,
Swimming in the pranks of dreamy coughs, the ride was wattage,
  steaming.
We caucused like electrons, our *trouble,* our *banter,* our titles of
  lithe and elation,

Through the *rehash* and the *yee-haw,* through digressions of
  zoo-ee-yooo, spewing for art, for the fit and the fat.

CIVILIZATION IN THE NEXT WAR

—1997

We didn't want to smell the underside of leaves
Out near the sand and the draining rage.
All we knew, overhead, muffled, badly sketched,
Were clouds, like lips, steeped in mist. Serenity
Meant standing with terrible strangers, waiting in line for a train.
Most days so little time to work the last nicotine-
Oiled intimate streets. Who could ever forget
The choral summers, tight-lipped, like steel?
Children still stripped to their underwear,
Happy as tall grass, and ran in the watery universe
Spewed from a broken main—how they laughed
With their grandparents looking tense, squinting, looking on.
The water plunged and shot—the children
Swung like dolls—in and out of the puddles,
The light like metal in the eye. Who said it was a phony war?
Sure as the body must break before it can feel,
The rhododendron exploded. The blooms rattled
And flared over the picket fences and the thick
Perennial brick-beds. Just living felt evil.

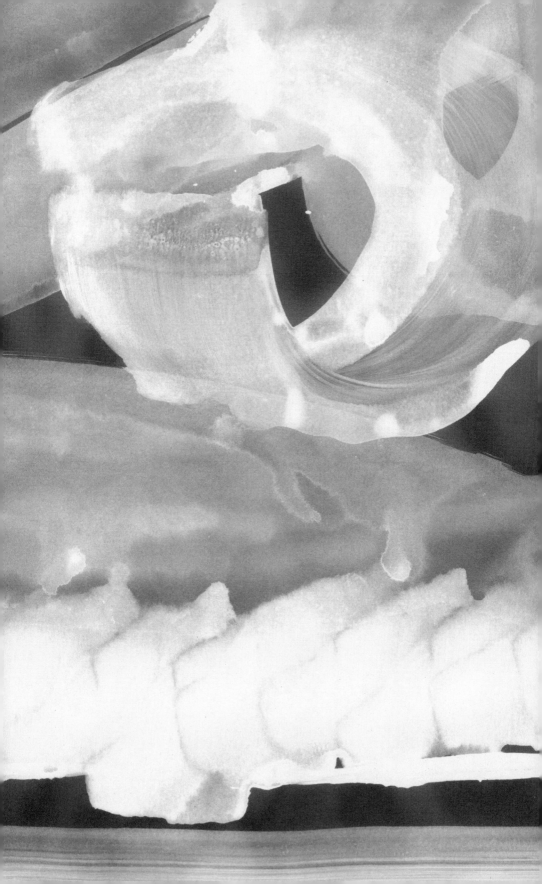

HOME

Fen

—*after Caryl Churchill*

One thing I've never said is *I'm selling the farm.* What's it like to
    be the fresh thief of glory?
I've said, *See you.* I've said, *The old man must be dead.* Out on this
    deaf fen a knife is a fiend.
I've stomached a beetle's stabs. I've seesawed with saints, burnt
    with my own sins.
Tigers haven't slashed my shell nor rode like an Eskimo on my
    sledge. Each year I tithe my ire

With tins to rattle at crows. I've been beaten like a tub, but didn't
    perish. My liver could verify it.
Frightened in the head, a rider of hens, as if my only rival were
    the first to be hanged in this parish,
I've got a coffin lined up and paid for. That's what this cough
    costs, sharper than a rasp.
I've gained by drifting, fed on figs, dug onions in squalls and the
    wrath of leering faces.

That's when the earth is awake, thawed and raw, without a ghost
    of a brass band near, quiet-like, for the dead's sake.

Mount Tabor

Slanted rain on the east side of the river, below the dormant
      mountain: Here, in a place I never knew
As a child, the old women sit with their knitting and pluck yarn
      as if stripping
Feathers off a chicken. Or, other days, dog-earing their
      Corinthians, their Job and Solomon's Songs,
They sing of slaughter, decaying birds, and the silent speech that
      flies, like a summer, all over the world.

Neither day nor night reverses aging gardens
Forgotten in the footnotes of expert treatises on time. Even
      lovers who walk along the emptied volcano
Know this is how it started: words and love, like roses, for hands
      or tombs. It'll never end,
So now when the children come and, without pain, picnic in the
      grass, the old women watch them as if in a changeless dream

That, even late in life, having passed though many doors,
      imprisons them, with faith, afresh.

Travels

Late in the summer a toy ship digresses in the grass, all its oomph
   mulling under a constellation of dandelions.
Its captain keeps not a log of travels, but pages of oneiric nights,
   numinous as harpoons and isinglass.
What would the old masters make of a sky of yellow petals? Or
   how to gad the sailors, those orphans of every region
Of sand and mountain and forest? How to grip the light? How to
   gnash? How to snare?

It's late in the summer. A toy ship perches at the end of the
   landscape of the lawn. It longs for some corsage of adventure
   among sirens and griffins.
The on-board priest is an Ezra. A lasso for wandering men to
   catch their necks in: his prayers.
You can hear him hum to the tune of olive trees that are only
   good for doing nothing,
Like a house with no ambition but to be a shelter, to allow
   longing, loving, and a little instruction,

To permit the children to play in the yard in their season of grass,
   to run, uninterrupted, small and slight, for hours.

Podunk

There was no way out. The dog-gone gripper was an enigma.
 Born in the mixed-nerve of county wind,
Born in the harp and hoarded early-service light, I came to trust
 ruddy dystrophies and kabalistic mediums.
Even in the climbing madness of the cyclorama, called Daily
 Living—with its diddering roll calls and lush royalties—
Even in the late afternoon bowls of chili (wolfed down to the
 tune of rum), I hedged when it came to the high road,
 citified as grammar.

Behind the henna, I would hear the inconvenient gossips say Nay
 to pork rinds and excuse the novelistic
Tyrants at the dump who, sometimes, at the end of their uncon-
 trollable Mazurkas, headed toward the muddy oil-fields
And bragged on being ladies' men and yelled, then turned pale,
 then blank, until carted off
With a diadem of empties at their feet and dibs on pastoral
 aliens. Later, heading home with the faith of pickups,

They would tune into the papacy of reinvention, and underneath
 their pleated breaths they would flunk again at love.

AMICHAI 1924–2000

We're standing outside a house I haven't built,

On a Jerusalem sidestreet, near a checkpoint to the Old City,

And the city itself sways like a vessel on the sea of longing.

There's laundry hanging on the roofs, the undershirts from one
    family

Waving like flags

Close to the bras and panties of their enemies.

His two arms are trembling, he says, *Lot's wife, you know, no
    looking back.*

When he speaks it sounds like singing,

And the tune is like a camouflage his mother dressed him in

To go to kindergarten. I say, *May heaven have pity.* He says,
    Amen.

All along he's out of breath,

Half the time in this life, half in a resurrection of sleeplessness.

He has the look of a man who's still waking up and running to
    meet an appointment—

Even now with Halevi and Ibn Ezra, and other poets

Dead a thousand years, and the dead of future wars,

And with his mother and father, and a line of comely women,

Each with a Leah's veil over her face, and her hair tied back with
    the sorrow of flowers,

Each with her palms turned up, each like a tent to lie down
    under.

He asks *What is the life span of death?*
As if at a hotel asking about the check-out time. Then, suddenly
Outside the house, amid the sand and dust of dream,
There's the sound of children's feet
Like the sound of wind, like the sound of *god begin.*

HERMES

And yet I was so unlike the others, the young Turks and kaffiyeh-
 draped factotums
Saying *You All* in their cool way and flying tourist class inside a
 cage of fireproof wigs.
Hephaestus used up drachmas for his ardent spirits and tossed by
 numbers. His joy stick
Worn to the nerve. Always a mix-up: not the judge but the jester,
 not the lowborn

But the nursling. The ripped, the unripped, the unripened, the
 wide spreading.
And always, too, the marching choirs, off-key on the Lord's Day,
Breaking into trochal patterns at half time. I'll skip the spa for
 despots and triumvirates
Who sneak seconds from the griddlecakes. To hell with inheri-
 tance. Let the trustees mix a tour de force.

All the drama I want is to be a turf man among green-helmeted
 horses. And, whenever possible, to be late to things.

ACKNOWLEDGMENTS

Thanks are due to the editors of several periodicals and anthologies for first publishing the poems cited here: *Agni Review* ("Amichai 1924–2000"); *American Literary Review* ("Kazoo," "Pagan"); *Denver Quarterly* ("Mushrooms"); *Fence* ("Explication de Texte," "Xerxes"); *The Journal* ("The Widow Bird Trip"); *Nimrod International Journal of Prose & Poetry* ("Epileptic," "Fen"); *Orion* ("After the Wedding"); *Poetry* ("Demarcation"); *The Sunday Oregonian* ("Civilization in the Next War," "Shoulders," "Travels"); *Zyzzyva* ("Third Generation Immigrants" as "Brawls"); *Cabin Fever: Poets at Joaquin Miller's Cabin, 1984–2001* [Word Works Press] ("Mount Tabor"); and *The New American Poets: A Bread Loaf Anthology* [University Press of New England] ("After the Wedding" [reprinted], "Under a Blossoming Plum Tree").

I'm grateful for the support of a fellowship from the National Endowment for the Arts and assistance from the Regional Arts and Culture Council, and I'm grateful to Karen Braucher and the staff of The Portlandia Group, publisher of the chapbook *Pilgrims & Beggars,* in which some of these poems also appeared.

I wish to say what a pleasure it has been to work with Linda Bierds, Gretchen Van Meter, and the staff of the University of Washington Press.

ABOUT THE POET

PHOTO BY TRICIA SNELL

David Biespiel was born in 1964 in Tulsa, Oklahoma, and grew
up in Texas. He is the author of *Shattering Air* (BOA Editions).
A contributor to *American Poetry Review*, *Poetry*, and *Parnassus*, he also writes the "First Sunday on Poetry" column for
The Oregonian. Biespiel has taught at the University of Maryland, Portland State University, and Stanford University.
He now teaches at Oregon State University and is writer-
in-residence at "the Attic." Past awards include the Wallace
Stegner Fellowship in poetry and the National Endowment
for the Arts Fellowship in literature. He lives with his wife
and son in the Hawthorne district of Portland, Oregon.

ABOUT THE TYPE

The poem titles are set in 18 point Syntax, a typeface designed by Swiss typographer Hans Eduard Meier (1922–). Syntax was first issued by the Stempel foundry in 1969 and remains one of the best unserifed romans ever made. The roman is a true neohumanist sans serif, based on Renaissance forms. In the late 1990s Meier did a subtle redesign.

The text of the poems is set in 11/18 point Minion, a typeface designed by Robert Slimbach (1956–), an American type designer, and issued by Adobe in 1989.

The typesetting was done by Suzanne Harris at Integrated Composition Systems in Spokane.